This book is dedicated to Aline, William
"Bras de Fer" and Thomas Bjorn "Ironside"

The author of this book Benjamin James Baillie
lives and works in Normandy

THE LAST VIKING

King Harald III "Hardrada" the hero of a thousand battles

1015 – 1066 A.D

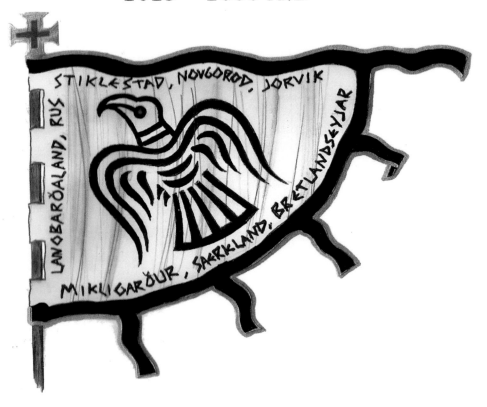

By Benjamin James Baillie

Contents

Introduction

King Harald "Hardrada" (the Ruthless/hard council) of Norway was one of the last great warriors of the Viking age. In a career that lasted over 30 years he fought in nearly every corner of the known world, from the cold lands of the Viking "Rus" (Russia) to the sun drenched shores of Sicily in the service of the Byzantine Emperor's personal bodyguard (the Varangian guard). In 1066 A.D the hero of a thousand battles embarked on his final campaign to conquer the Kingdom of England, which would decide the fate of the Island of Britannia.

Quote from Harald's saga (Heimskringla) Snorri Sturluson

"Where the battle storm was ringing, where arrow cloud was singing, Harald stood there, of armour bare, his deadly sword still swinging."

Homeland of the Vikings, Scandinavia (The Norwegian Fjords)

Fairhair dynasty

In 1015 A.D a boy called Harald Sigurdsson later "Hardrada" was born into the Fairhair dynasty. Harald's great, great grandfather Harald "Fairhair" Halfdansson fought a bitter series of campaigns in the late 9th century to unit the Viking peoples of the Western part of the Scandinavian Peninsula.

In 872 A.D at the battle of Hafrsfjord near Stravanger (Norway) Fairhair crushed the petty chieftains of Sognefjord and Rogaland. This victory enabled Fairhair to become the first legitimate King of the new nation state of Norway.

Many of the defeated rebels refused to accept the central authority of Fairhair and fled Norway to seek refuge abroad.

Sverd i Fjell monument commemorating the Battle of Hafrsfjord, Stavanger, Norway

One of the most famous Viking nobles to flee was Rollo/Hrolf, the Walker who eventually became the Roujarl (Count of Rouen) and founder of the Duchy of Normandy in Northern France.

Towards the end of Fairhair's reign he co-ruled with his son Eric I "Bloodaxe" until his death in 933 A.D. The Norwegian crown passed onto his children and grandchildren, who fought both internal enemies and external threats from Denmark and the other Viking powers in the region.

Saint Olaf "King Olaf Haraldsson" 1015 – 1030 A.D

Olaf Haraldsson (later St Olaf) was a great, great grandson of Harald Fairfair. After his father's death in the late 10th century, Asta his mother remarried Sigurd Syr, another relative within the Fairfair dynasty. They had five children together including the youngest named Harald (later Hardrada).

When Olaf reached adulthood he left the family home and joined one of the Viking raiding armies that were terrorising Europe. He learnt the deadly art of Dark Age warfare in the Baltic before heading on to seek his fortune in Anglo-Saxon England.

Thorkell's attack on England

Olaf joined Thorkell "the Tall" attack on England in 1009 A.D. The huge Viking army ravaged East Anglia and Southern England. At Ringmere / Hringmaraheiðr in Norfolk the invaders were confronted by the Anglo-Saxon forces under the command of Æthelstan (King Æthelred the Unready son in law). As the two armies clashed together, Viking berserkers hacked their way into the Saxon shield wall.

St Olaf statue, St Magnus Cathedral, Kirkwall (Orkney Islands)

Then according to the Anglo-Saxon chronicle, Thurcytel "Mares head" (a descendant of Danish origin) fighting for the Saxons fled the field. Whether or not he collaborated with Thorkell's Vikings or simply crumbled under the pressure is unclear. As Thurcytel's East Anglian men retreated from the field, the Vikings used their superior numbers to annihilate the remaining Anglo-Saxons. Æthelstan and the men from Cambridge fought on and refused to yield fighting until the last man. By the end of the day the slaughter was complete with Æthelstan and the other Anglo-Saxon nobles lying dead on the field of Ringmere. With local resistance crushed, Thorkell sacked Thetford and Cambridge before heading south to ravage the Thames valley.

In 1011 A.D Thorkell's Vikings laid siege to Canterbury. Unable to breach the defensive Roman walls they were eventually assisted by the treachery of Ælfmaer who let them into the city.

Once inside the Vikings went on the rampage and sacked the city. Ælfheah the Anglo-Saxon Bishop of Canterbury was captured and taken prisoner. He forbade anyone to pay his ransom and after several months the Vikings grew tired of their holy prisoner. In a drunken rage the Bishop was put to death in a violent way.

Runestone U344, Orkesta churchyard (Sweden). Commemorates the adventures of Ulf of Borresta who was a Viking warrior in Thorkell's army.

Anglo-Saxon Chronicles reported:

"After being seized he was shamefully put to death. The Vikings pelted him with bones and ox-heads, then one of them struck him on the head with the back of an axe, so that he sank down with the fatal blow"

After three years of plunder and warfare the invaders were finally bought off with the Danegeld (bribe / protection money) from King Æthelred the Unready.

Normandy

Olaf parted company with Thorkell and with his share of the spoils decided to cross the English Channel and head for Normandy "Land of the North-men". The Viking colony of Normandy had only been in existence for just over a century, but it was still welcoming Viking raiders to either settle down and farm the land or join the Dukes feudal armies as mercenaries. Olaf sailed down the 150 kms of the river Seine towards the Norman capital: Rouen. The fertile Seine valley which had been devastated by the Vikings was now in a state of reconstruction and prosperity. The great stone abbeys of St Wandrille and Jumièges dwarfed all the thatched dwellings around them and would have demonstrated the power of the Duke and the Church as Olaf passed by in his dragon headed long ship. As Olaf's ship docked in the harbour of the capital he would have been greeted by Scandinavian, French and traders from a variety of places. Rouen was one of the principle trading ports of the Viking world and goods such as amber from the Baltic to slaves were all traded in the bustling streets of the capital.

St Olaf flag of Normandy

Olaf entered into the service of Duke Richard II as a mercenary and participated in the Duke's campaigns against Odo (the Count of Blois and Chartres). Olaf and his men were dispatched to Normandy's southern border with Brittany. In a spectacular raid he captured the border town and castle of Dol. When a Breton relief force arrived to retake the town, Olaf carefully prepared the battlefield by secretly digging trenches and holes to thwart the advance of the Breton cavalry. As the armoured knights charged towards Olaf's shield wall they were stopped dead in their tracks by the hidden trenches and traps. Knights were thrown from their horses and then fell prey to Olaf's men who finished them off using Dane axe, sword and spear.

Rouen Cathedral crypt, Normandy, Olaf and the Viking warlord Rollo were both baptised there almost a century apart.

According to the Norman chronicler William de Jumièges on his victorious return back to Rouen Olaf was baptised a Christian in the great cathedral (1014 AD). Olaf may not have been a devote Christian, but he was shrewd enough to understand that Christianity could be used to gain more power for the monarchy and also help to centralise Norway.

At the Norman Ducal court Olaf heard the story of Frankish King/Holy Roman Emperor Charlemagne who had united most of Western Europe under his control. So impressed was Olaf that he later named his royal long ship 'Karlshöfði', after Charlemagne.

The Return to Norway

In 1015 A.D Olaf left Normandy and set sail via England to return home to Norway. His objective was to continue the work of his great, great grandfather and unit the country under his Kingship. Since the death of King Olaf Tryggvason at the battle of Svolder in 1000 A.D Norway had been under the nominal control of the formidable Danish King Sweyn "Forkbeard" and his allies the Jarls of Lade.

In 1014 A.D Forkbeard died only a few weeks after being crowned King of England. His son Canute decided to follow his father's footsteps and tried his luck to gain the English crown. This gave Olaf the opportunity to launch his expedition to become King of Norway. Olaf returned back to his family home and sought the support from his stepfather Sigurd Syr. Sigurd warned Olaf of the dangers he faced, but decided to back his stepson and persuaded the other petty Kings of the Upper-lands to support him. In the following year Olaf defeated the rebel forces arrayed against him at the battle of Nesjar. This victory secured the throne for Olaf who became King of Norway.

Olaf's half-brother Harald "Hardrada"

According to the Heimskringla Saga Olaf feasted with his mother and step father Sigurd. He was introduced to his half brothers and sisters, Guthorm, Halfdan and the youngest Harald. In a ruse Olaf pretended to become angry so to test the character of the children. Guthorm and Halfdan sought the refuge of their mother, while Harald grabbed Olaf's beard and refused to show fear. Olaf responded by telling Harald:
"You will be vengeful one day my brother".

From an early age Harald looked up to his half-brother King Olaf and wanted to become a great Viking like him.

After ten years of trying to impose central order and Christianity upon his people Olaf was forced to flee Norway and seek refuge in the Viking colony of the "Rus" in modern day Russia.

By 1030 A.D Olaf was ready to return and reclaim his throne. The young Harald was now 15 years old and ready to experience his first battle at his half-brother's side.

First blood, the battle of Stiklestad 1030 A.D

After marching across Sweden and through the mountains, Olaf entered the Verdal valley and took up position at Stiklestad farm some 50 miles from Trondhiem. On the 29th of July 1030 A.D King Olaf arrayed his forces on the high ground with young Harald placed on his flank with the loyal men from the Upper-lands. He planted his personal banner of a serpent deep into the ground for all the rebels to see he was there in person.

Although heavily outnumbered, the King decided to attack the rebels who were commanded by Kalv Arnason, Tore Hund and Harek on Tjotta. The Royalist army charged down the slope shouting out the war cry "Forward men of the King, men of Christ and the cross". The rebel army buckled from the steer force and momentum of the charge. King Olaf in a furious frenzy burst out from behind the shield wall, hacking down all in his path. After the initial shock, the rebel commanders began to re-organise themselves and use their superior numbers to push back and then surround the King's men.

First Olaf's standard bearer was cut down, and then the King's close companions were picked off one by one in the vicious hand to hand combat. Thorstein Knarresmed plunged his axe deep into the King's leg before being killed by one of Olaf's bodyguards (Finn Arnason). As the King struggled to regain his balance using a large rock Thore Hund stabbed him in the belly with a spear, then the final blow came from Kalv Arnason who struck the King in the neck with his sword. Whether or not Harald saw his half-brother killed is unclear, but according to the Heimskringla saga he was rescued from the carnage by Rognvald Brusason (later Earl of Orkney). The injured Harald was taken by Rognvald to a safe house where he recovered from his wounds.

In time Harald covertly made his way through Sweden with a small band of exiles, taking ship to the safe haven of the Kingdom of the "Rus" (Russia).

The death of King Olaf, Battle of Stiklestad
29th of July 1030 AD

Exile: in the land of the "Rus"

By the mid-8th century armed Viking traders were heading across the Varangian Sea (Baltic Sea) and setting up small colonies to trade with the native Slaves in modern day Russia. Viking merchants joined together to protect themselves from the sometimes hostile tribes of the Russian steppe and became known as Varangians, which in old Norse means; var = oath/pledge. The Varangians infiltrated the great inland river systems of the Volga, Dvina and Diepner to trade in furs and amber from Finland and the Baltic region to silver from the Islamic world. Trade flourished and some settlements became large towns and cities such as Novgorod and Staraja Ladoga (Russia).

In 862 A.D a group of Varangians called the "Rus" (Finnish name for Sweden) led by Rurik gained control over Novgorod and founded the Rurik dynasty. According to the Russian primary chronicle Rurik was invited by the native peoples of the Slaves, Chuds and the Krivichians to rule over them.

"Our land is great and rich, but there is no order in it. Come to rule and reign over us"

When Harald arrived at the port of Staraya Ladoga in 1030 A.D the "Rus" were engaged in various wars against the Chuds and the Pechenegs. Prince Yaroslav welcomed the arrival of the Norwegian warriors and quickly recruited them to fight for him as mercenaries. Harald entered into the service of Prince Yaroslav and was send straight into action against the Chuds (a tribe from modern day Estonia).

In the brutal campaign Harald and the Varangian mercenaries led by Eilif crushed the resistance of the Chuds. Fresh from their victory, the Varangians advanced with the "Rus armies into Poland and captured several cities.

After the campaign in Estonia and Poland, Harald was sent to bolster up the defence of the "Garðaríki" (a chain of defensive forts near Novgorod). In 1032 A.D Harald ventured north to the very edge of the "Rus" Kingdom near the Ural Mountains. The expedition to the Pechora River introduced Harald to the fierce Finno-Ugric tribes who inhabited the inhospitable Arctic north.

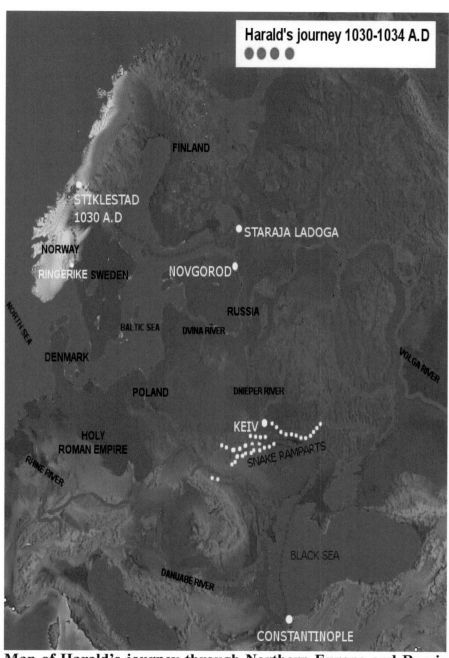

Map of Harald's journey through Northern Europe and Russia 1030-1034 A.D

The fortress of Staraja Ladoga, one of the first Viking settlements if Russia

After returning from the cold Ural Mountains, Harald was probably involved in the re-settlement of Polish and Chuds captives along the fortified settlements of the river Dnieper. This would have brought him into contact with the Pechenegs. The Pechengs were a nomadic warrior race much like the Huns before them who inhabited the Russian Steppe. They had been in conflict with the "Rus" and were a constant threat to merchants traveling on the trade routes to Constantinople and the Islamic east. The "Rus" had been building a series of forts and earthworks known as the "snake ramparts" to combat the Pecheneg menace.

The snake ramparts were over 100 kms long south east of Kiev. Harald would have been very familiar with these forts and would have provided armed escorts along the trade routes towards the Black sea. Slowly he rose in respect and standing amongst the "Rus". So much so that he even asked for the hand in marriage of Elizaveta (Prince Yaroslav's daughter).

Harald fighting on the Russian Steppe

According to the Flateyjarbok (Icelandic Saga) although Harald was of Royal blood and an heir of the Norwegian crown his demand was rejected until he could offer her great wealth and prestige.

Constantinople and the Varangian Guard 1034 A.D

With this in mind instead of attempting a return to Norway Harald decided on heading south to seek out fame and fortune in the light of the world and capital of the Byzantine Empire, Constantinople. Since the fall of the Western Roman Empire in the 5th century A.D Constantinople had taken up the mantle of civilization and defender of the Roman world. For over five centuries the Byzantines had battled against countless enemies including the Huns, Visigoths, Sarassids and Arabs to remain one of the world's greatest superpowers.

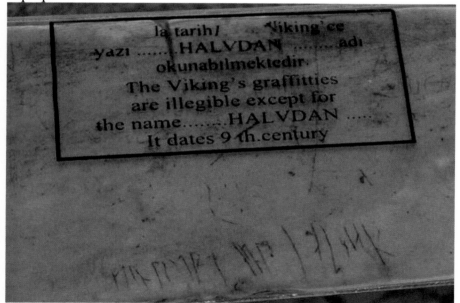

The famous Halfdan inscription, Viking rune graffiti, probably written by a Varangian guardsman (Hagia Sophia)

In the late 10th century the Byzantine Emperor Basil II concluded an alliance with the "Rus" ruler Vladimir I (Prince Yaroslav's father). As part of the treaty the "Rus agreed to convert to Christianity and also send several thousand Varangian mercenaries to fight for the Emperor.

In a series of campaigns with the help of the Varangians Basil II crushed the internal rebellions and restored order within the Empire. For their great courage and fierce fighting spirit Basil created the Varangian Guard. They became the Emperor's elite bodyguard and were mostly made up of Scandinavian warriors when Harald arrived in 1034 A.D Byzantine policy had tried to discourage men of Royal blood from entering the Varangian guard. Harald managed to conceal his identity and entered into imperial service under the pseudonym of Nordbrikt.

The destruction the Arab pirates

As in Russia Harald was sent straight into action against Arab pirates who were terrorising the Mediterranean and Aegean Seas from their bases in Sicily, North Africa and Asia Minor. The Scandinavian Varangians were of particular use to the Byzantines for their renowned skill as great seafarers. Bolstered up with the experienced Scandinavian Varangians, the Byzantines took to the open water and hunted down the corsair vessels. For extra motivation the Varangians were given the rights of extra plunder.

For every pirate ship captured an agreed percentage went back into the imperial coffers and the rest could be shared amongst the Varangian crews. After countless naval skirmishes the pirate menace was destroyed using Greek fire and the cold hard steel of the Varangian battle axes and swords.

Harald's saga (Heimskringla) Snorri Sturluson

"Harald sailed around the Greek islands and caused great damage upon the Arabs corsairs"

Serkland (land of the Saracens) 1035 A.D

In a follow up campaign Harald and the some of the Varangians were recruited into the army of Constantine (the Strategos of Antioch and also the Emperor's brother) to destroy the inland pirate bases of Asia Minor (modern day Turkey). According to some of the sagas Harald captured many towns in Serkland. If this information is true then Harald would have been attached to General Georgios Maniakes, who was spearheading the Byzantine revival in the east.

The re-conquest: Sicily 1038 A.D

With a renewed confidence the Emperor Michael IV decided to turn his attention to the Western Mediterranean. Sicily and Southern Italy had been re-conquered from the barbarians in the 6th century by the Byzantine generals Belisarius and Narses.

In the centuries that followed Byzantine power had waned in the region. This allowed the Saracens to capture the strategically important island of Sicily. With the pirate menace eliminated, Michael IV gathered together some to the finest troops in the Empire, including Harald's Varangians to retake Sicily.

In the late summer of 1038 A.D the invasion force commanded by General Georgios Maniakes landed in Italy and headed for the straits of Messina. The Italian Lord of Salerno (Guaimar IV) had been asked by the Byzantines to provide military assistance for the assault on Sicily. Guaimar accepted the call to arms and sent a detachment of Lombard's and some 300 troublesome Norman mercenaries to join the expedition.

The rugged mountainous coastline of Sicily

In a lightning strike Harald's Varangians were the first troops to land on the shores of Sicily and secure a beachhead. After brief resistance the important port of Messina was taken. Harald's Varangians advanced inland with the Byzantine armies and according to the Heimskringla saga he was prominent in capturing several Citadels.

Harald's guile; the capture of the Sicilian Citadels

In four spectacular episodes Harald is said to have devised a series of devious plans to capture some of the most strongly fortified towns in Sicily.

(The Birds plan) Heimskringla saga:

"Harald noticed birds returning to their nests in the castle walls and roofs. At once he ordered a large number of them to be captured. Upon this act they had splinters of tarred wood attached to their backs. The tare was then set alight and the birds released. Immediately they returned to their nests and fire engulfed the castle and town. After a short time the defenders surrendered".

(Uninvited wolves) Heimskringla saga:

"There was another Citadel which Harald had come with his army. The city was both well defended and so strong, that there was no hope of beseiging it. The castle stood upon a flat hard plain. Harald decided to dig a passage from a place where a stream ran in a bed so deep that it could not be seen from the castle. They threw out all the earth into the stream, so it be carried away by the water. At this work they laboured day and night; while the rest of the army cut off the city from the outside world. When Harald perceived that his underground tunnel was so long that it must be within the city walls, he ordered the Varangians to arm themselves. At dawn they entered into the passage and at the end of the tunnel they dug above their heads until they came upon stones laid in lime which was the floor of a stone hall. The Varangians broke open the floor and rose into the hall.

There sat many of the City's garrison eating and drinking, and not in the least expecting such uninvited wolves; the Varangians instantly attacked them with sword in hand, and killed some, and those who could get away fled. The Varangians pursued them; and some seized the City's gate, and opened it. The Byzantines at once quickly overwhelmed the defences and entered the City. The people of the Citadel fled, but many asked for quarter from the troops, which was granted to all who surrendered. In this way Harald gained possession of the City and found an immense booty in it."

(The third City ;The Icelanders Ulf and Haldor) Heimskringla saga:

The third Citadel, was thus far the greatest and strongest of them all, and also the richest and most inhabited. Around the City there were great ditches, so evidently it could not be taken by the same ruse as the former. Harald pretended to stand down his troops, making the City's garrison believe that there would no immediate attack. When the garrison saw this they became bolder, drew up their array on the City walls, threw open the castle gates, and shouted to the Varangians, insulting them and jeering at them to attack , and telling them to come into the City, and that they were cowards and not fit for battle. Harald told his men not to take the bait and pretend to play games, but secretly prepare to assault the City. Harald choose two of his close companions, Haldor and Ulf from Iceland to lead the assault. Both were very strong men and bold under arms. Several days passed the City's garrison showed more courage, they would go without weapons upon the City's wall, while leaving the gates wide open. Haldor and Ulf observed this and instantly seizing their weapons, they made at for the City's gate. Haldor and Ulf had no shields, but wrapped their cloaks round their left arms. The Icelanders fought off the garrison and managed to keep the gates open until Harald and the main body of the Varangians arrived. When Harald came to the gate his standard-bearer fell, Harald told Haldor to take up the banner. Haldor replied "Let the Trolls pick up the banner, you coward", But these were words more of anger than of truth; for Harald was one of the boldest of men under arms.

The battle was hard fought, but Harald and the Varangians took control and captured the City. Haldor was badly wounded in the face, and it gave him great pain for as as long as he lived.

(The false funeral) Heimskringla saga:
"The fourth Citadel which Harald beseiged was the greatest of all we have been talking about. It was so strong that there was no possibility of directly attacking it. The Varangians surrounded it, so that no supplies could get in or out. Harald pretended to fall ill, and he took himself to his bed. He had his tent put up a short distance from the main camp. His men went usually in companies to or from him to hear his orders; and the City's garrison observed this activity and sent out spies to discover what was going on. When the spies came back to the Citadel they told the elders that the commander of the Varangians was ill and not expected to recover. Harald then sent out false reports that he was dead. Some of the Varangians were sent to the City to ask the priest's to allow their fallen leader to be burried in the City's Cathedral. The Clergy were very eager to get the corpse, knowing that upon that there would follow very rich gifts. A great many priests, therefore, clothed themselves in all their robes, and went out of the City with cross, shrine, relics and formed a beautiful procession. The Varangians also made a great burial. The coffin was borne high in the air, and drapped over with a linen banner. All the time a well and breathing Harald lay inside with several swords waiting for the right moment to strike. When the Varangian coffin bearers arrived at the gates of the Citadel they placed the coffin right across the entrance, keeping the gates open. Harald burst open the coffin lid and quickly distributed the hidden swords. The Varangians went on the rampage and killed everyone before their feet, whether holy or unconsecrated. The City was taken and its wealth distributed amongst Harald and the Varangians."

The Sicilian landscape and stout resistance of the Saracens slowed down the progress of the conquest. After two years of bloody fighting, only the Eastern part of the island had been brought under Byzantine control. In 1040 A.D at the battle of Troina the Saracens were utterly defeated.

The Byzantines attacked in three divisions with the crack troops of Harald's Varangian Guard and the Norman shock cavalry under the command of the De Hauteville brothers (William and Drongo) leading the assault. William achieved fame and gained the nickname "Bras de fer"/ iron-arm for killing the Saracen Emir in single combat.

Maniace castle, Sicily, named after the Byzantine General George Maniakes

The battle of Troina and the capture of Syracuse marked the high water point of the re-conquest of Sicily. Soon afterwards a dispute broke out over the spoils and plunder. The Heimskringla commented that many soldiers left their units to join Harald's Varangians when they learnt of the booty being shared out under his command. Indeed the Varangians although under Maniakes command were in a privileged position as they swore their oath of loyalty to the Emperor alone.

Unable to punish Harald, Maniakes decided to make an example of the Lombard commander Arduin. Arduin had been sent by his men and the Norman contingent to remonstrate about the pay and allocation of the plunder. General Maniakes had him arrested and severely beaten for his impertinence.

William de Hauteville "Bras de fer / Ironarm"
Harald's comrade in arms in Sicily

This action caused the Normans and Lombards to abandon the expedition and return to Southern Italy. The General's fall from grace continued when he insulted the commander of the imperial fleet. As a result he was relieved of his command.

Italy 1041 A.D

On his return to Southern Italy Arduin was determined to avenge his treatment at the hands of the Byzantines. In secret contact with the Normans of Aversa he fomented a rebellion to overthrow Byzantine power in the region. Within months the revolt spread and even the great city of Bari fell to the rebels. In response the Emperor sent a new commander (Michael Dokeianos) to stabilise the deteriorating situation. According to the skald Thjolf, Harald's Varangians were recalled from Sicily and ordered to help put down the revolt on mainland Italy.

The Norman stronghold of Melfi (Southern Italy)

Harald had to fight his former comrades in arms, the Normans and Lombard's. Apart from small references from the scalds we know near to nothing about his involvement in the fighting. The Imperial campaign did not go according to plan; although Bari was recaptured the forces of the Catepan (Byzantine commander) were defeated at the Battle of Olivento near Melfi.

In 1041 A.D the Byzantines suffered another catastrophic defeat in the Ofanto valley. Although outnumbered, the Normans and their Lombard allies attacked and routed the Catepan's army near Cannae. Whether or not Harald took part in these disastrous encounters is unclear. Harald's Varangians are more likely to have been withdrawn and sent back to Constantinople to participate in the Emperor's war against the Bulgars.

Harald "the Burner of the Bulgars"

The Bulgars were a semi-nomadic people similar to the Huns and Pechenegs. From the 7th century onwards they migrated west and settled in modern day Bulgaria, Macedonia and the Balkans. In the late 10th /early 11th century the Byzantine Emperor Basil II (creator of the Varangian Guard) waged a vicious war to force the Bulgars to accept his authority.

Emperor Michael IV based on a coin relief

In the final great battle of the war at Cimbalingus/Kleidion, 1014 A.D the Bulgars were decisively defeated. In retribution for the death of the Byzantine General Botaneiates some 15,000 prisoners were rounded up and divided into groups of one hundred men. Then 99 men in each group were blinded, leaving one man to guide the others home.

The defeated Bulgars begrudging accepted the over lordship of the Empire until 1040 A.D when Peter Deljan proclaimed himself King of the Bulgars. The rebellion gathered pace and many towns and cities in Northern Greece and Macedonia fell to the Bulgars. The Emperor Michael IV mustered the Byzantine forces in Constantinople and set out to extinguish the Bulgar menace once and for all. Michael IV led an army of some 40,000 men in person and ravaged the Bulgar homelands.

The Skald Thjolf reported that Harald fought many battles and called him the "burner of the Bulgars". As part of the Emperor's elite troops he would have been in the thick of the fighting. After a year of brutal warfare the Bulgars were defeated and their leaders either killed or captured. Harald and the Varangians returned with the Emperor in triumph to Constantinople. It was the high point of Harald's career in the Varangian Guard; he was also promoted to the rank of Spatharokandidatus.

The fortifications of Constantinople overlooking the Bosphorus

Coup d'état Constantinople 1041-1042 A.D

The Emperor Michael IV's health had been failing even before he led the campaign against the Bulgars. On the 10th of December 1041 A.D he was given his last rights before dying. John the Orphanotrophos (Michael IV's brother) had been the power behind the throne for the last few years of his brother's reign.
On the death of the Emperor he proclaimed his nephew Michael V as the new Basileus/Emperor. Michael was determined not to be controlled by his overbearing uncle John the Orphanotrophos. In a lightning strike John was arrested and sent into exile.

Michael wanted to distance himself from the old regime; first he pardoned and restored to power the disgraced General George Manazikes. The General was then ordered to return to Italy and re-conquer the territory lost to the Normans and Lombards.

In the spring of 1042 A.D Michael decided to remove his adopted mother and Co-Empress Zoe. Some senior members of the Varangian Guard including Harald were also arrested and thrown into prison under the pretext of defrauding the imperial treasury. This decision may have been a political necessity in order to neutralise any potential military threat from the Varangians whose loyalty remained suspect. Michael's coup d'etat had been executed swiftly, but the reaction of the populace in Constantinople had been badly misjudged. Large crowds gathered in the imperial center and ordered that Zoe be returned to power. Although Zoe was brought back, the mob could not be appeased. Soon the unrest engulfed the entire city. Harald's luck changed when according to the Heimskringla saga;

"A lady of distinction with her servants came and brought ladders and ropes to the tower where Harald was imprisoned. They lowered ropes and hauled Harald and his companions out".

Harald quickly gathered the loyal Varangians under his sacred raven banner and headed for the church of St John of the Studion where the Emperor and his uncle Constantine were holding out. Michael V and Constantine were dragged out from the sanctuary of the church and roughly handed by the angry crowd.

When Harald and the battle hardened Varangians arrived on the scene they restored some sort of control before been ordered to punish the Royal prisoners. The skald Thjolf reported that Harald took charge and personally blinded the Emperor himself.

Harald's saga (Heimskringla) Snorri Sturluson:
> **"He who the hungry wolf's wild howl,**
> **Quits with prey, the stern, the fell,**
> **Midst the uproar of shriek and stout,**
> **Stung the Emperor's eyes out,**
> **The Norse King's mark gives cause to mourn,**
> **His mark the Emperor must bear,**
> **Groping his sightless way in fear"**

The gruesome night's work had been done with ruthless efficiency. Michael V and Constantine were carried off into exile and a new regime was proclaimed in the name of the Empress Zoe and her sister Theodora. Zoe married her former lover another Constantine who became the new Emperor Constantine IX.

Escape from the Empire

Harald's recent spell in prison and the unpredictable nature of Byzantine politics may have influenced his decision to leave the guard and return home to Norway. Another reason may have been reports that Prince Yaroslav of the "Rus" was planning an attack on the Byzantine Empire. Harald must have had conflicting interests as since the start of his career as a Varangian mercenary he had been regularly sending his spoils of plunder back to Russia for safe keeping. If he stayed in Constantinople and fought against Yaroslav he would have certainly lost his well-earned treasure and also any prospect of marrying Elisaveta / Ellisif (Yaroslav's daughter).

The iron chain of the Golden Horn, Harald encountered a similar chain on his escape from Constantinople in 1042 A.D

After the coronation of the new Emperor Constantine IX Harald asked to leave the service of the Varangian Guard. His demand was refused for Constantine needed his best troops for the forthcoming struggle against the "Rus". He probably was more concerned about the prospect of Harald giving sensitive military information to Prince Yaroslav. Harald was watched by the Emperor's spies, but on an evening in late summer he made a daring escape from Constantinople. Together with a chosen band of loyal Varangians Harald commandeered two imperial ships.

Under the cover of darkness the two ships laden with plunder and provisions headed out towards the gateway of the harbour. Only the great iron chain lay between them and their break for freedom. As Harald's ship neared the chain he ordered the either crew to head to the back of the ship, thus transferring the weight to allow the ship to pass over the chain. The plan worked perfectly and Harald's ship entered the Black sea. The second ship did not get off so likely and got stuck on the chain, backing its back before sinking into the deep waters of the Borphorus. After picking up the survivors and salvageable goods from the wreckage Harald headed north across the Black Sea and into the mouth of the river Diepner.

Princess Elisaveta of the "Rus"

Princess Elisaveta

Harald sailed up the great rivers of the Russian steppe towards the heartland of the "Rus". On reaching Kiev in the bleak winter of 1042 A.D he was greeted with a rapturous reception. It had been 8 years since the almost unknown warrior had left to seek out fame and fortune. Now he returned with a fearsome reputation and a huge fortune in gold and plunder.

The Golden Gate, Kiev built by Prince Yaroslav in the 11ᵗʰ Century

Snorri Sturluson (Harald's saga) reported that;

"Harald took into his possession all the gold and precious things which he had sent from Constantinople. Together it made up a vast treasure that no man had ever seen before in the Northern lands"

Prince Yaroslav was pleased to see Harald and an agreement was reached between the two concerning the hand of Yaroslav's daughter Princess Elisaveta. During the Christmas celebrations Elisaveta and Harald were married. Harald and Yaroslav talked in depth about the planned "Rus" campaign against Constantinople. Harald provided information, but he would not participate in person for he wanted to return home to Norway.

Norway 1030-1045 A.D

After the Battle of Stiklestad in 1030 A.D King Cnut the Great of Denmark and England decided to place his son Sven Cnutsson as ruler of Norway.

Cnutsson arrived in Norway along with his mother Ælfgifu and continued to impose the centralisation and authority of the crown upon the Norwegian nobility. With the backing of Cnut's military resources, the Norse nobles had no choice but to lay low and begrudgingly accept Cnutsson's rule. In 1035 A.D King Cnut died and with him the great North Sea Empire.

Norway re-asserted its independence and two of the former leaders of the rebellion against King Olaf, Kalv Arnason and Einar Tambarkjelve decided to travel to Russia and bring back Magnus (King Olaf's illegitimate son). They traveled across the Varangian Sea (Baltic Sea) and pleaded with Prince Magnus and the exiled nobles to return home and reclaim the Norwegian crown.

King Magnus I "the good"

In the autumn of 1035 A.D Magnus, his close companions including Rognvald Brusason and his father's former enemies set sail to oust Cnutsson.

On arriving in Sweden they sought the help of the Swedish King Anund Jacob. Together they raised an army and invaded Norway. With Magnus's army swelling by the day and his authority crumbling around him Cnutsson and Ælfgifu were forced to flee the country and seek refuge in Denmark. At the age of only 11 years old Magnus was proclaimed King of Norway. Over the next five years Magnus consolidated his position and took the war to Denmark. In 1040 A.D a peace conference was arranged between King Magnus and the Danish King Harthacnut.

It was agreed whoever died first would inherit the others Kingdom. In 1042 A.D Harthacnut died and Magnus became King of Denmark. Although gaining victory at the Battle of Lyrskov Hede in 1043 A.D Magnus's authority was challenged by Sweyn Estridsson/Ulfson (a nephew of King Cnut the Great). Sweyn and Magnus went to war, but by 1045 A.D a more menacing shadow loomed over Scandinavia in the form of the last great Viking Harald "Hardrada"

Return of the last Viking

Harald left the "Rus" port of Staraja Ladoga and headed for Sweden. He was welcomed there by King Anund Jacob, who was the uncle of his wife Elisaveta.

In Sweden Harald encountered Sweyn Estridsson. The two warriors joined forces and gathered a great army to attack Magnus of Norway. Harald was eager to carve out a Kingdom for himself and believed that he had a better claim to the throne of Norway than his nephew Magnus. In a good old Viking tradition Harald and Sweyn went "a Viking" and raided the Danish coast. The islands of Fyn and Zealand were ravaged by Harald and Sweyn's marauding Vikings.

Heimskringla saga:

> **"Harald, thou have laid waste to the island,**
> **The Zealand men away have chased,**
> **The wild wolf by daylight roams,**
> **Through their deserted silent homes,**
> **The fury of his wasting hand.**
> **Helms destroyed and shields broken"**

Harald's tactic apart from gaining plunder and provisions was to show the people that Magnus could not protect them. King Magnus concerned by the events on the Danish coast ordered a general levy in Norway to combat his uncle's unfriendly behavior. Rather than risk a total war against Harald and Sweyn, Magnus was convinced by his advisers to send emissaries to negotiate a peace treaty.

An accord was reached in which Harald agreed to give Magnus half his fortune for half of the Kingdom of Norway. While the secret negotiations were taking place it seems Sweyn got wind of the plan. The two allies were now at loggerheads and during a drunken night's feast Harald and Sweyn argued. According to the Heimskringla saga Harald retired to his ship. During the night fearing treachery he changed beds and placed a log in his billet. In the middle of the night an assassin crept aboard Harald's ship and struck Harald's suspected billet with an axe. The axe embedded itself deep into the log and the assassin hurriedly escaped into the darkness. On uncovering the attempted assassination Harald ordered his men to make sail and head for Norway.

Two Kings One Kingdom, Norway

On his arrival in Norway Harald was met by his nephew King Magnus. To two kinsmen greeted one another and

Ratified the treaty in which Harald became the co-King of Norway. Harald for his part of the bargain brought his vast wealth of treasure into the great hall and handed half of it to Magnus. The magnitude of gold was so immense that even Magnus who was King of Norway and also Denmark could not compete. After the peace celebrations Harald returned home to the Upperlands of Norway. During the winter of 1046 A.D Harald and Magnus collected taxes and men for the fore coming campaign against Sweyn Esdridsson. In the summer of 1047 A.D the two King's gathered together an almighty host and invaded Denmark. Their objective was to capture or kill Sweyn Estridsson and force the Danish nobility to accept their rule. In an incident, Harald's ships arrived in Denmark before Magnus and he moored his vessels in the royal berth, normally reserved for the King. When Magnus arrived he was extremely upset. Harald backed down and ordered his men the find another place within the harbour. Harald then boarded Magnus's ship and the two rulers nearly came to blows over the dispute. It was clear that Harald was too big a character for the peace to last indefinitely. The two King's parted company and scoured Denmark in search of Sweyn. Faced with a battle he could not win, Sweyn fled the country and took shelter in the Oresund region of modern day Sweden. During his tour of Denmark Magnus was taken ill. His health deteriorated and on the 25th of October 1047 A.D he died.

King Harald III "Hardrada"

The shock and early death of Magnus left Harald as sole ruler of Norway and disputed King of Denmark. Harald wanted to march on Viborg and use the Norse army to force the Danes into accepting his overlord-ship, but Einar Tambarskelve refused to take part in the campaign and convinced many of King Magnus's retinue it was their duty to return to Norway and bury Magnus. With a large part of the Norwegian host abandoning his army, Harald had little choice but to follow suit and return home. On hearing of Magnus's death and Harald's departure, Sweyn headed back to Denmark and was proclaimed King Sweyn II.

Overleaf: depiction of the invasion of Denmark →

Sweyn is reported to have said:

"So help me God, I shall never yield Denmark."

Back in Norway Harald (now King Harald III of Norway) buried his nephew and commenced preparations for his plan of resurrecting Cnut's "North sea Empire". In order to realise his dream, he had to destroy Sweyn's power and authority in Denmark. In the summer of 1048 A.D the Norwegian fleet under Harald raided the Danish coast. The villages and settlements along the coast near Godnarfjord were burned to the ground and the local population terrorised. After a successful raid, Harald returned home where the King's spies brought word that Sweyn was constructing a powerful fleet and planned to attack Norway to avenge the raid of 1048 A.D.

The Battle of Gaut Elf River 1049 A.D

Sweyn sent word to Harald to either agree to peace or to settle the dispute by a pre-arranged battle. Harald never a diplomat agreed to the pre-arranged battle, which was due to take place on the Gaut River (border between Denmark and Sweden) during the following summer.
Harald's fleet of over 300 ships sailed to the Gaut River in the summer of 1049 A.D.
To his dismay Sweyn and Danish fleet was nowhere to be seen. Harald feared that Sweyn had tricked him and was probably already raiding Norway. He decided to send back most of the Norwegian levy and continue on a raiding mission along the Danish coast. With his remaining sixty ships Harald attacked the great Danish trading port of Hedeby. Situated on the German border, Hedeby was one of the principal marketplaces of the Viking world.
In the devastating attack Hedeby was completely destroyed and ransacked. The destruction was so great that the town never recovered from the Norse assault.

Heimskringla Saga:

"All Hedeby is burnt down, Strangers will ask where stood the town ".

The Haithabu Viking museum, Hedeby (photograph euro-t guide.com)

Harald's men loaded their ships with the spoils from the raid and also a number of Danish slaves and hostages. Content that the raid had paid for the entire campaign, Harald set sail and prepared to return back to Norway. Near the tip of Jutland, Sweyn's army appeared on the coastline. He challenged Harald to do battle, but Harald realising he was seriously outnumbered counter challenged Sweyn to a sea battle. Harald sailed on but a change in the wind and heavy sea fog forced him to anchor his ships off the Isle of Hlér. As the fog lifted on the following morning Harald and his crews were met by a terrifying sight, Sweyn's entire Danish fleet was sailing straight for them. The King immediately ordered his men to ready the ships oars and row as fast as they could. Heavily laden with the spoils from the Hedeby raid, Harald's ships were no match for the Danish longboats who were cutting the distance between the two fleets. Taking the initiative Harald told his men to make the ships lighter by throwing overboard the plunder and anything else not of use.

The Danes were still gaining on them, but Harald in a last ditch attempt to escape ordered the Danish captives to be thrown overboard. As the hapless men, women and children were swimming for their lives in the cold Baltic waters, Sweyn ordered a halt to save his compatriots from a watery death. Harald escaped back to Norway by the skin of his teeth.

Hardrada "hard council / the ruthless"

Back in Norway Harald set about strengthening the power of the crown. He had not forgotten the way Einar Tambarskelve had withdrawn his support back in 1047 A.D. Einar had been a major power player in Norwegian politics for nearly half a century.

He had fought at the Battle of Svolder in 1000 A.D and had been a major opponent of King Olaf Haraldsson/ Saint Olaf (Harald's half-brother).

Einar had seen Kings come and go and he believed that Harald would be no different. On ever occasion he flaunted the King's laws and openly challenged royal authority at the (Thing) meetings. In one such act of defiance he brought with him 8 warships packed with over 500 hundred men to a council meeting. Harald had seen enough and was determined to destroy the power of the old lenderman.

Harald is reported to have said that he could not remain King of Norway until Einar "Kisses the thin mouth of the axe"

Einar Tambarskelve depicted on the Melhus coat of arms (Norway)

When one of Einar's men was arrested for stealing, he was brought before the Thing at Niðarós (Trondheim) to be tried. Einar protested and tried to break up the proceedings at the Thing using his armed men. He agreed to meet King Harald and discuss the situation, but Harald had decided to rid himself of Einar for once and for all.

Einar came to the King's great hall with his son Eindridi and a retinue of armed soldiers. He told Eindridi to wait outside while he met with the King. As he entered the inner chamber, Harald's bodyguards surrounded him and hacked him to death with their swords and battle axes.

Eindridi rushed into the great hall to try and save his father, but it was too late for Einar was lying in a pool of blood in front of him already dead. Harald then ordered his men to dispatch Eindridi in the same way as his father.

Although Einar's men tried to break into the hall, leaderless they broke off the fight and fled the scene. With two fatal swoops of the axe Harald had destroyed the power of the Tambarskelve's. Over the next ten years, Harald crushed all resistance against him. It was during this period in Norway that he gained the nick-name "Hardrada" meaning ruthless / hard council.

An old enemy, Kalv Arnason

Next on Harald's vengeance list was Kalv Arnason, the murderer of Harald's half-brother Saint Olaf. Although Kalv had been pardoned by the King and had returned from exile, his days were numbered. During the annual raid on Denmark in 1051 A.D Harald placed Kalv in command of the landing party during the attack on Fyn Island. Kalv led his men off the long ships to secure a beachhead for the main force under Harald. The Danes decided to attack Kalv's war band before Harald could land his men. After some vicious hand to hand fighting Kalv was slain and his men annihilated. Kalv's brother Finn believed that Harald had delayed the landing of the main force, knowing full well that without support Kalv's men had no chance of surviving. Whether true or not Harald had accomplished the objective of ridding himself of his half-brother's murderer. Shortly after the event Finn Arnason fled Norway and joined forces with Harald's enemy King Sweyn of Denmark.

The heir to the Tambarskelve's power in the unruly Upperlands region of Norway was a certain Hakon Ivarsson. Hakon was appointed Jarl by Harald who hoped to pacify the region and secure the young Jarl's loyalty. Hakon remained loyal to Harald, but his position as Jarl and figurehead to the Earls of Lade caused the King to be suspicious of Hakon's long term ambitions.

Over the next few years Harald continued the work of his predecessors to unify and strengthen royal power in Norway. He married Tora Torbergsdatter who was actually related to both Finn and Kalv Arnason. With this union Harald hoped to break the political opposition of some of his opponents and also secure a male heir for his line. During Harald's reign more churches were built including the completion of St Olaf's and St Gregory in Nidaros. The future Norwegian capital of Oslo, although not created by Harald actually became more prominent during his war against Denmark.

Prow of the Skidbladner, reconstructed 9th century Viking ship (Unst, Shetland Islands) Shetland Amenity Trust

The Battle of Nisa 1062 A.D

By 1062 A.D both Harald and Sweyn of Denmark were seeking a final showdown. In the ten years or so of endless fighting between the two countries, the economies of both Norway and Denmark had suffered immensely. Harald sent a challenge to Sweyn to meet him on the Gaut Elf River to decide the issue once and for all. Sweyn gladly accepted and readied the Danish fleet for action. In the summer of 1062 A.D Harald's fleet set sail from Oslo with his flagship the "Long Serpent"/ Drekamum at its head. On arrival at the Gaut Elf River Sweyn's ships were nowhere to be found just as before in 1049 A.D.

Harald once again sent home part of his fleet to protect Norway, but this time kept over 150 ships with him just encase Sweyn tried to ambush his force. As the Norwegian fleet sailed into the Laholms Fjord Sweyn fleet was spotted. Many of King Harald's senior commanders urged the King to flee as the Danish fleet was double the size of the Norwegian flotilla. Harald would have none of it, and this time he was determined either to destroy King Sweyn or die in the process.

Heimskringla Saga:
"Sooner shall all lie dead upon one another than I flee"

The King organised his fleet into battle formation with the "Long serpent" in the centre. He placed Jarl Hakon and the men from Trøndelag on the flanks. In the mouth of the Nissa River the two fleets collided into one another. Many of the ships on both sides had being roped together, making huge mobile fighting platforms. The Norwegian and Danish soldiers and sailors engaged one another in the bloody hand to hand combat aboard the dragon headed vessels. Men were butchered and drowned in their hundreds. Jarl Hakon disengaged his ships from the formation and attacked the Danish flanks.
His action caused panic and confusion amongst the Danes who were now being attacked from both sides. The battle raged into the night and Harald could be seen using his bow to deadly effect.

Heimskringla Saga:
"The Upperland King was all the night, firing arrows' to deadly flight"

Harald fought his way aboard the Danish flagship looking for King Sweyn. The King was nowhere to be found and Harald had to content himself with capturing Sweyn's personal banner and effects. As Jarl Hakon attended to the battle wounds of his men a small boat came alongside his ship and asked for help. A hooded man approached Hakon and whispered:

Heimskringla Saga:
"I would accept my life from you if you would grant it to me"

The stranger asked Hakon to be taken to the shore to which Hakon agreed. When the Jarl returned to the heart of the battle in the morning and boarded Sweyn's ship he was told that Sweyn had escaped or been drowned. Hakon knew better, as the stranger he had saved during the night was none other than King Sweyn. Harald gathered up his forces and returned home triumphant to Norway.

The Battle of Vanern, the end of Jarl Hakon

During the victory celebrations Hakon was revived as the hero of the battle. Rumours then reach Harald's ears that Hakon had saved and put to shore a cloaked stranger during the battle. The rumours were collated and it became common knowledge that this person was King Sweyn. Harald was furious and ordered the arrest of Jarl Hakon.

The Jarl had already left and returned to the Upperlands when word reached him that King Harald's men were in hot pursuit. In the middle of the night Hakon fled into the forest just as the King's men arrived at his house. He then crossed over the border and sought sanctuary in Sweden. Although the Upperland region was in near revolt and its inhabitants refusing to pay their taxes, Harald had to turn south and attend a peace conference which had been brokered between emissaries from Denmark and Norway. After over a decade and a half of brutal warfare Harald relinquished his claim to the Danish crown. Peace with Denmark allowed Harald to turn his attention to the rebellious Upperlanders and their figurehead Jarl Hakon. The King's spies brought word to him that Jarl Hakon was amassing an army of Norwegian dissidents and Gotlanders (Swedes) to overthrow him from power. Harald was galvanised into action, he too gathered together his forces and decided to take action against the rebels in a pre-emptive strike. The King's army assembled at Kungahälla on the border between Norway and Sweden. The Heimskringla saga comments that Harald's army carried their vessels overland through the forests and around the Trollhatten waterfalls until they reached the great lake of Vanern. Harald's scouts located the rebels who were now also aware of the King's forces in the vicinity. The final showdown took place somewhere on the eastern shores of lake Vanern. Harald formed his heavily armoured huscarls into battle formation on a ridge overlooking the enemy positions.

Jarl Hakon whom Harald knew to be an impatient man ordered his men and the Gotlanders to advance towards the Norwegian position. Flurries of snow drifted down and the cold wind blew in the faces of Hakon's advancing soldiers. When they reached the foot of the ridge, Harald gave the signal to charge down the hill.

The sheer momentum of the armoured huscarls punched a hole straight through Hakon's ranks. Harald's professional soldiers hacked their way towards Hakon's personal war banner, which once belonged to King Magnus.

As the light faded the destruction of the rebel army was complete. Hakon escaped the carnage and is said to have retrieved his banner by ambushing the Norwegian army on their victorious return home. The Jarl retreated into the wilderness never to be seen again. For Harald the victory at the Battle of Vanern secured his throne from any serious internal threats against him. During the winter of 1064 A.D he exacted his revenge on the communities of the rebellious Upplanders with brutal retribution. Some were maimed, others killed and all were punished for deifying King Harald III "Hardrada".

Lake Vanern, Sweden

The last campaign, England 1066 A.D

Free from internal opposition in Norway Harald turned his attention west, towards the Kingdom of England.

Harald had a claim to the English throne dating back to the agreement made between his nephew King Magnus and King Harthacanut.

Harthacanut was King of Denmark and also England. The treaty concluded in 1040 A.D stipulated that whoever died first would inherit the others Kingdom. When Harthacanut died in 1040 A.D Magnus became King of Denmark. Although he also claimed England, the Anglo-Saxon council "the Witan" decided to elect their preferred candidate Edward, son of Æthelred II "The Unready" from the Royal line of King Alfred the Great. Magnus decided against waging war to pursue his claim, which lay dormant for another 25 years.

On the 5th of January 1066 A.D King Edward (known as the Confessor) died. His death sparked a deadly power struggle between three of the most fearsome warriors in Western Europe: Harold Godwinsson (the Earl of Wessex), William "the Bastard" (the Duke of Normandy) and King Harald III of Norway "Hardrada". In the cold icy homeland of the Viking world Harald decided the time was right to launch the greatest gamble of his career and force his claim to the England crown. Fearing another foreign King, the Witan immediately elected Harold Godwinsson as King of England. Their decision caused outage from William of Normandy and Harald "Hardrada", who both began preparations for a full scale invasion of Anglo-Saxon England.

Harald's ally, Earl Tostig

Tostig Godwinsson was the brother of King Harold II (Godwinsson) of England. During the reign of Edward "the Confessor" Tostig had been made Earl of Northumbria on the death of Siward (The Viking Earl of the region).

After several years of Tostig's heavy handed rule the Northumbrians rose up in revolt and marched on the city of York. Once inside they rounded up Tostig's supporters and massacred them. They then declared Tostig an outlaw and sent for Morcar, brother of Edwin Earl of Mercia to take over the Earldom. At Northampton the rebel Northumbrians were met by King Edward's representative, Harold Godwinsson (the Earl of Wessex). After prolonged negotiations Harold agreed to the rebel demands and Tostig was replaced by Morcar as Earl.

At the royal council meeting Tostig was officially stripped of his title. In a furious rage he accused Harold, his own brother of instigating the northern rebellion against him.

For his outburst Tostig was exiled from the Kingdom. He took ship with his remaining supporters and fled to his wife's homeland of Flanders in modern day Northern France/Belgium. On the death of King Edward "the Confessor" in January 1066 A.D Tostig hoped that Harold would recall him back to England and restore him the Earldom of Northumbria. Harold was in no position to do this as to strengthen his claim to the throne he had married Edith, the sister of both Edwin and Morcar. This union was the last straw for Tostig who knew that unless there was a regime change in England he would never regain his title.

In the spring of 1066 A.D with help from his brother in-law Count Baldwin of Flanders, Tostig harried the Southern coast of England. He attacked the Isle of Wight, but was forced to retreat when Harold (now King Harold II) sent a large force to intercept him. Sailing around the coast Tostig unsuccessfully tried to get his brother Gyth to join his cause before landing in Lincolnshire. Tostig ravaged the county, but was decisively defeated by Earls Edwin and Mocar.

Forced to flee yet again, Tostig decided to seek the support of a foreign power. He first made contact with King Sweyn Estridsson of Denmark. Sweyn who had only just recovered from his war with Norway was unwilling to provide any military support.

The former Earl then travelled to Viken where King Harald "Hardrada" was keeping his court. Harald was not convinced and is said to have told Tostig that the Norsemen (Norwegians) have no desire to conquer England and that the English could not be trusted. Tostig seems to have convinced Harald that many of the English nobles would gladly welcome him as King and that England was ripe for the taking. Harald always an ambitious man agreed to the plan and called out a general levy in Norway.

The invasion of England and the Battle of Fulford

During the summer of 1066 A.D Harald assembled a colossal fleet of over 300 ships and 10,000 men. He crossed the North Sea and landed in Shetland before continuing onto the Orkney Isles to gather further troops. The Norse fleet then sailed down the Scottish coast and joined the smaller force of Tostig near Tynemouth.

Together they continued south and raided Cleveland. At Scarborough Harald's Viking army came ashore and sacked the town. This was a deliberate act to terrorise the local population into submission. As the town burned and the sky filled with black smoke from the thatched houses, Harald headed into the mouth of the Humber estuary and up the river Ouse. The greatest Viking invasion of England in living memory was underway; at Ricall they disembarked and headed for the capital of the north, York (Jorvik in Old Norse). On the 20th of September at Fulford just outside York Harald's men were confronted by an Anglo-Saxon army under the command of Earl Edwin of Mercia and Earl Morcar of Northumbria.

The walls of York and gatehouse of Micklegate bar

Harald formed up his army into battle order, the left flank resting on the river and the centre and right wing along a parallel ditch. The King ordered his famous land-ravager flag to be brought forward and placed deep into English soil. The Earl's men advanced and spotted that the Norse army was weakest on their right flank. They ordered the whole Saxon army to concentrate their attack on the ditch section. The fierce Saxon charge smashed straight into the Norse formation, axe, spear and sword were all used to deadly effect in the unrelenting combat. Encouraged on by their initial success, the Saxons broke through the Norse ranks. At this crucial moment, Harald the hero of a thousand battles entered the fray. He ordered a general charge with the land-ravager flag carried before him. His best troops and Viking berserkers pushed Edwin and Morcar's men back into the ditch, where many were slain.

Some Norse troops may have also outflanked the Saxon position by crossing the marsh via the old Roman road. The battle turned into a rout and by the time the Saxons were in full retreat, the ditch was so full with bodies that the Norse could cross it without getting their feet wet.

Heimskringla Saga:
> **"Brave Harald drove along.**
> **Flying but fighting the whole way.**
> **At last, demoralised, they could not fight.**
> **And the whole body took flight and fled".**

Both Edwin and Morcar escaped the carnage of Fulford, but the Norse victory caused a general panic back in York and much of Northern England. Harald had won a great victory which strengthened his claim to gain the English crown. He advanced to the very gates of York and received the surrender of the Northern capital. The city was spared the dreaded sack, but was ordered to send hostages to a designated rendezvous point several miles outside the city at a place called Stamford Bridge.

The Battle of Fulford commemoration plaque, outskirts of York

The last battle, Stamford Bridge

After the submission of York, Harald returned to his ships at Riccall. On the 25th of September 1066 A.D the King marched out back towards Stamford Bridge, leaving a large proportion of his army at Riccall under the command of his son Olaf and Eystein Orre.

←Overleaf, the Battle of Fulford, 1066 A.D

Overconfident and believing that the English had been utterly defeated Harald allowed many of his men to leave their heavy armour and mail coats with the fleet. When they arrived at Stamford Bridge they could see clouds of dust swirling up into the sky. Harald asked Tostig who it could be and the Earl replied that it was probably English friends and allies coming to submit and join the Norse army. Tostig was completely wrong, and it became clear when they saw the "Fighting man banner" of Wessex that it was the full military might of Anglo-Saxon England under the command of King Harold Godwinsson. After the news of the invasion, King Harold had marched north and covered the some 200 miles from London to York in lightning speed.

As the English army approached Harald had little choice but to stand his ground and hope to delay the battle until his main force could arrive from Riccall. He sent some messengers on horseback at full speed to gather the remainder of the Norse army to join him at Stamford Bridge. Harald was caught completely unaware, yet only one battle stood in his way of re-uniting the great North Sea Empire of King Cnut. He organised his outnumbered and lightly armoured troops into a circular shield wall formation with the sacred Land-Ravager flag in the center.

Then twenty riders came forward from the English position. One of them asked if Tostig was in the army. When Tostig replied that he was, the rider said that he had a message from King Harold.

The message was that if he deserted the Norse he would be re-instated as Earl of Northumbria and also given a third of the Kingdom to rule. Tostig replied what would be given to King Harald "Hardrada" for his trouble, to which the rider answered.

"Seven foot of English soil, for he is taller than most men"

As the English rode back to their lines Hardrada asked Tostig if he knew the man who had spoken so gallantly. Tostig said he did and that was King Harold Godwinsson himself. Harald observed to his close comrades;

"What a little man is Harold Godwinsson, yet he sat up well in his stirrups"

With the formalities at an end the Anglo-Saxons attacked and overwhelmed the Norse contingent stationed on the western side of the river. Their advance was checked by a lone Viking berserker who heroically defended the footbridge over the river Derwent.

With his gigantic Dane-axe he single handedly cut down over 40 English soldiers who challenged him.

Battle of Stamford Bridge commemoration plaque

The duel was ended when a Saxon warrior crept beneath the bridge and speared the berserker from below. As the giant Viking warrior fell to the ground the English shouted out a deafening battle cry and advanced towards the Norse position. There have been many theories as to why Harald did not defend the bridge and use it is a choke point until the arrival of the Norse reserves. As the most experienced and battle hardened warrior of his day he would have certainly have recognised this tactical advantage. The answer to this debate may be in the actual origin of the placename of Stamford. The Germanic origin of the word "ford" means a shallow river crossing. The river Derwent may have been exceptionally low due to the warm and dry weather conditions of 1066 A.D, allowing the Anglo-Saxon army to cross the river in force without needing to rely on the footbridge. According to the Heimskringla saga the English attacked on horseback. Although the Anglo-Saxons used horses like the Vikings for transport they are not known to have fought as cavalry, but if the sagas are correct this may have been a detachment of King Harold Godwinsson's royal huscarls. Harold had fought with Duke William of Normandy on campaign in Brittany and had been very much impressed by the Norman mounted cavalry. When he returned to England he created a unit based on the Norman mounted knight.

**Norse berserker at the Battle of Stamford Bridge
25th September 1066 AD**

The English threw everything at the Norse shield wall, but each assault was repulsed and thrown back. The green Yorkshire grass turned red with blood and the field was littered with the dead and wounded from both sides. Soon the lack of armour and overwhelming English numbers began to tell. At the crucial moment just like at Fulford Harald bust out from behind the shield wall and charged straight into the English ranks hoping the break the deadlock and turn the battle to his favour. The King flew into a violent berserker rage and hacked down everyone in his way.

No one could withstand the fury of his charge as he forced his way through the Saxons ranks infront of him. Harald's Norse charge nearly broke the spirit of the English who were being pushed back and on the verge of fleeing the field.

Then disaster struck "Hardrada" was hit by a stray arrow in the windpipe. The great warrior King was stopped dead in his tracks, dropping to the ground like a felled mighty oak tree. It was perhaps befitting that he died sword in hand "the Viking way" fighting until his last breath, the way he would have wished. Harold Godwinsson offered quarter to his brother Tostig and the remaining Norse soldiers, but they refused to surrender and fought on to the last man defending Harald's body and the sacred land-ravager flag.

The death of King Harald "Hardrada" at Stamford Bridge

Shortly afterwards Eystein Orri arrived on the battlefield with the Norse reinforcements from Riccall. Although exhausted from the forced march they entered the bloody battle in a furious rage. Taking charge of the raven banner they inflicted many casualties upon the English. After a short while they ditched their armour and shields in order to carry on fighting, but this made them easy targets for the English archers who decimated their numbers. As darkness fell on the battlefield the last great Viking army to assault England had been annihilated. Some of Harald's men managed to escape the carnage and return to Riccall with the land-ravager banner.

The victorious English King Harold made a peace treaty with King Harald's son Olaf, allowing him and the remaining Norse to return home back to Scandinavia. Only 24 ships out of over 300 were needed to take the Norwegian survivors home. So great was the slaughter of Stamford Bridge that piles of bones still littered the battlefield well into the 12th century. Harold's victory was short lived, for he also fell just week's later defending England against the Norman

invaders under Duke William of Normandy at the Battle of Hastings.

Harald's Landravager (Landøyðan) banner / Fairy flag

Harald's famous Land-ravager banner which had been with him since the Byzantine re-conquest of Sicily seems to have survived the battle of Stamford Bridge. After being recused by Eystein Orri's men from the blood soaked field it disappears from history, but there is a legend that it still exists today in Dunvegan castle on the Ilse of Skye in Scotland. Known today as the "Fairy Flag" it may have been brought to the Western Isles

(Which at the time were under Norse control) by a Viking warrior in Harald's army called Godred Crovan. The flag can still be seen on display within the castle.

After thirty years of countless battles and wars, King Harald III "Hardrada" died fighting on the blood soaked field of Stamford Bridge. A warrior hero until the end, he entered Valhalla and secured his place as the last great warrior of the Viking age.

Heimskringla Saga:

"He fell among us in the field.
The gallant men who saw him fall
Would take no quarter, one and all
Resolved to die with their beloved King,
Around his corpse in a corpse ring"

Other titles from the author:

THE GREAT HEATHEN ARMY

Ivar "the Boneless" and the Viking invasion of Britain"

THE PAGAN LORDS

The forgotten Viking campaigns of the Great Heathen Army in France and Spain 840 – 982 AD

"The Normans"

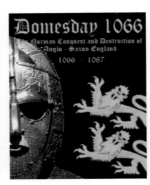

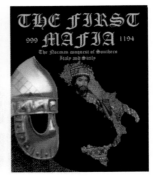

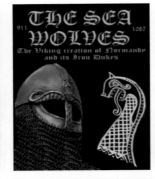

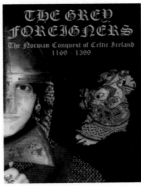

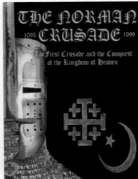

Printed in Great Britain
by Amazon